# De Pastor's Wife

# De Pastor's Wife
A Journey Beyond the Caribbean Skies

### Roxan Gardner

# A SPECIAL GIFT
## Just for you

**PRESENTED TO**

----------------------------------------

**FROM**

----------------------------------------

Copyright © 2024 Roxan Gardner

All rights reserved. No part of this publication may be reproduced in any form without prior permission of the publisher.

*Dedication*

*I extend my deepest gratitude to the Almighty God for His unwavering guidance and divine inspiration, which breathed life into every poem within the pages of this book.*

*To my beloved husband, Sam, your steadfast presence throughout the various phases of my life's journey has been a wellspring of support and an enduring source of love. Your encouragement has been a cornerstone of my creative endeavours.*

*To our son, Jemaule, your boundless ambition and remarkable intellect serve as a beacon of hope for your generation and an endless source of pride for us.*

*Last but certainly not least, my sister-in-law, Louise, a brilliant playwright in her own right, has been a well of inspiration, nurturing my passion for the dramatic arts and kindling my ever-growing love for the world of creativity.*

*With deepest appreciation, Roxan.*

## Table of Contents

Introduction.......................................................................8

Jonah the Runner............................................................11

Parkside Fellowship .......................................................16

Newbold - I Can't Believe It .........................................21

Leeds District .................................................................28

Unconditional Positive Regard .....................................34

Boy Chile ........................................................................39

De Pastor's Wife ............................................................45

Surprise Entry! ...............................................................55

Glossary..........................................................................62

About the Author ...........................................................64

## Introduction

I invite you to join me on a profoundly personal journey through the pages of 'De Pastor's Wife: A Journey Beyond the Caribbean Skies.' This book is an embodiment of my pride in my Caribbean/African heritage and my deep-rooted love for the vibrant language that colours our stories. As you turn these pages, you will not just be reading my words but sharing a piece of my heart.

Life took me from the lush shores of the Caribbean to the bustling streets of England, a transition that opened up a world of new experiences. The English language, the tantalizing aroma of unfamiliar cuisines, and the ever-changing weather all became a part of my daily life. Through this journey, I learned to embrace and cherish the differences, and to find beauty in the blend of cultures.

This book is my love letter to the rich culture of my native Antiguan/Barbudan dialect. It's a tapestry woven with stories and poetry; each thread spun from the experiences of my life in England. These are not just words on paper; but pieces of my soul laid bare. Each verse is a mirror in which you may see your own experiences, your transitions, and your journey.

In 'De Pastor's Wife: A Journey Beyond the Caribbean Skies,' you will encounter the stories behind each poem, a glimpse into the moments and emotions that inspired my verses. As a pastor's wife, I've witnessed the ebbs and flows of faith, and as a student, I've embraced the joys and challenges of learning in a foreign land.

The threads of Antiguan and Barbudan dialects run through these pages, connecting me to my roots while bridging the gap with my new home. I use this vibrant language to paint the pictures of my journey, inviting you to see through my eyes and understand the complexities of adaptation.
To my English friends, I extend a special invitation. These poems hold messages that resonate with the experiences we've shared. To my fellow Caribbean souls, you will find a piece of home in every verse, a connection that transcends ethnic origins.

Every poem is not just a creation; it's a memory, a feeling, a slice of life. The stories behind the poems are windows into my own experiences, my joys, my tribulations, and the narratives that have shaped my life.

Embark on this journey with me. Prepared to laugh, empathize, and discover that the human experience is a composition crafted from humour and hyperbole. These words are more than just expressions, they represent fragments of myself, reflecting life's beauty and complexities. So, come, let's explore the world through my eyes. Let's share stories, laughter, and emotions. This book is more than literature; it's an intimate sharing of a life lived with open arms and an open heart.

## Jonah the Runner

The story of Jonah has held a special place in my heart since I was a young girl. Its narrative is a captivating blend of excitement, intrigue, and spiritual reflection. The account of a man swallowed by a mammoth sea creature while attempting to evade the call of God, has always been a source of wonder and mystery.

As I've grown into adulthood, my fascination with Jonah's journey has only deepened. It's not just the extraordinary display of God's power that intrigues me, but also His remarkable ability to create a sea creature capable of swallowing a man whole. The themes of mercy and forgiveness that pervade the story continue to captivate my heart and mind.

However, my connection to Jonah doesn't end there. It extends into the life of my beloved husband, whose spiritual journey has been profoundly influenced by this very prophet. His undergraduate thesis delved into the depths of Jonah's tale, uncovering layers of meaning and spiritual insight. Jonah's struggles and his eventual surrender to God's calling reflect my husband's path to ministry. His story mirrors that of Jonah, as he initially resisted the divine assignment, and did everything in his power to run in the opposite direction. Ultimately, he too yielded, and today, God is using him mightily.

For the many months it took my husband to complete this scholarly work, the name Jonah became a constant theme in our home. Our conversations revolved around Jonah. My husband diligently crafted sermons about this enigmatic prophet, which I had the privilege of listening to. His work was academically rigorous and meticulously presented.

But as a layperson, I yearned for a deeper, more personal connection to Jonah's story. I sought a version of this remarkable narrative that I could relate to on a fundamental level. It was from this yearning that the idea to create a poem about Jonah was born.

I wanted to express the essence of Jonah's story in a language that resonated with me. This poem is the culmination of that endeavour, an attempt to present this timeless tale in a way that is deeply personal and relatable. It is an exploration of Jonah's character, a man whose experiences offer profound lessons in faith, surrender, and the boundless grace of our Creator.

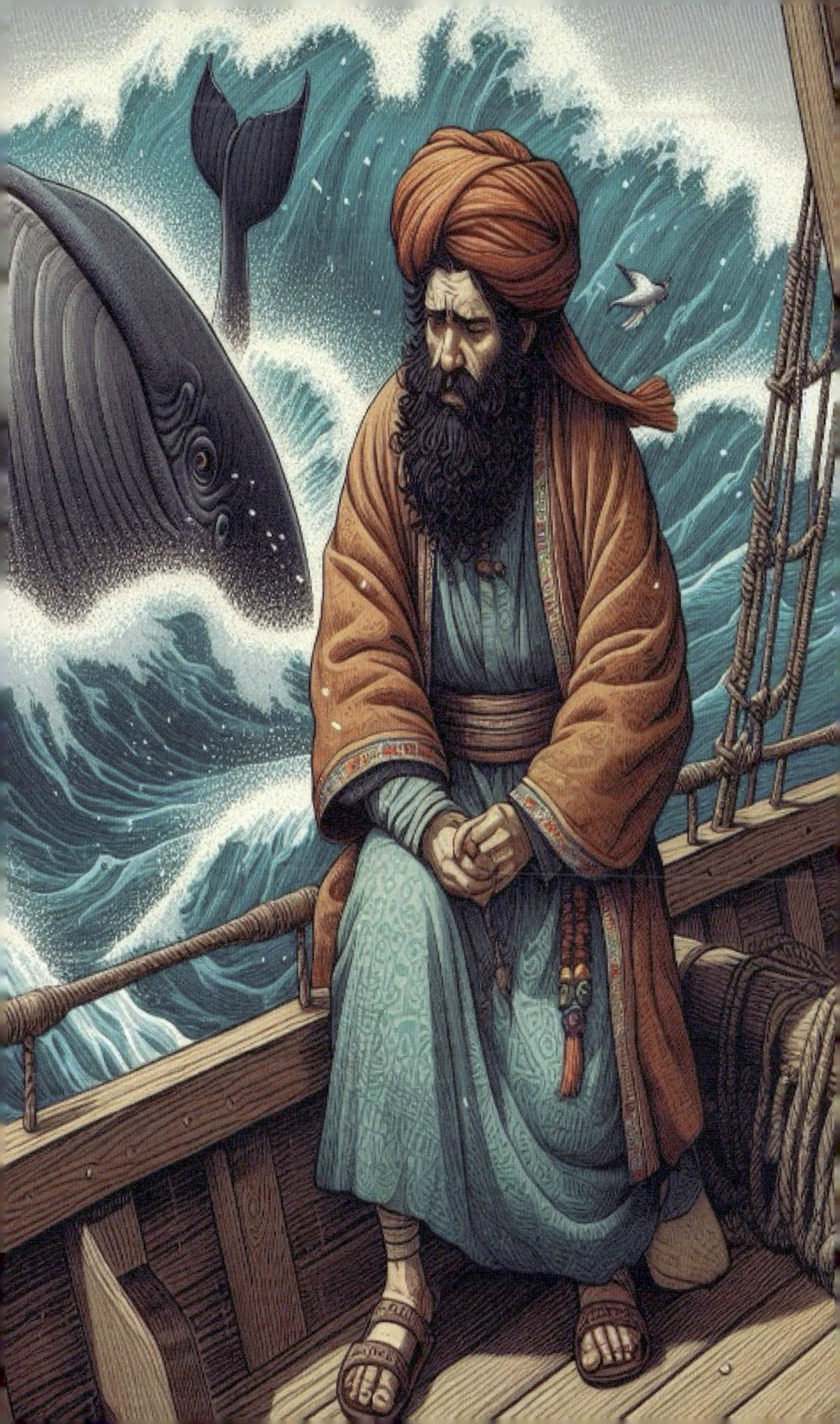

If I were to present this poem to His Majesty – the King, I would introduce it along these lines...

Long ago lived a prophet by the name of Jonah
He was summoned by God to deliver a message to the people of Nineveh
It was a task that Jonah did not foresee
Hence it was a mission he thought of most disagreeably

Jonah decided on a plan of escape
That would take him in a direction opposite to his mission's mandate
He boarded a ship and thought he was free
But my dear Jonah, this thing was not meant to be...

But, to add the Caribbean flavour to the story of Jonah it would read something like this...

Bredrin, a go tell you de story bout breddar Jonah
Him was call to save de people of Nineva
Jonah say "Gad? ...not me sa"
Dem people wicked dem mus suffa

Him jump pan wan boat but all was in vain
De vessel start rocking like it in a hurricane
De sailors dem fraid and start fu wonda
A who mek we get all this lighting an thunda?

Right away dem wake up brother Jonah
But man, you a sleep when all this happening?
You better let we know if something you hiding
Dem say let every man pray to de Gad dem kno
To stop de boat going two and fro

Jonah confess, that it might be he
You a get all this trouble because a me
De men dem sorry but dem na wa fu dead
So dem decide fu throw Jonah overboard instead

Jonah bawl "Lawd, me sorry you see"
So God cause a big fish fu swallar he
Up pan de shore him come fu lan
Jonah run to Nineva as fast as him can

So let this be a lesson fu all to see
Dat God is merciful but na mek joke wit He
If He can let a fish swallow one big man
When you hear God call, you better respan.

## Parkside Fellowship

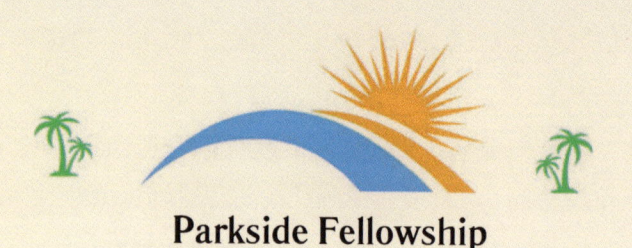

Parkside Fellowship, during the period of our attendance, was a remarkable congregation. Although not officially organised as a church, it was steadily growing in numbers and purpose. It was a place where people of all ages found not just a spiritual home but a profound sense of purpose.

This fellowship was unique in the way it catered to every age group. From the youngest children to the seasoned elders, there was a place for everyone. It wasn't merely a place of worship but a place to engage, connect, and serve.

At the heart of the community was the idea that everyone could find a ministry that resonated with their passions and talents. It wasn't just about traditional roles within a church; it was about unleashing the potential of each individual. Whether it was participating in a sports league, engaging in tract distribution, volunteering in community outreach, or contributing in some other way, there was a role for everyone.

What set Parkside Fellowship apart was its unwavering focus on soul-winning, a mission driven by a shared commitment to spreading faith, love, and goodwill. Everything, every activity, every program, was designed to reach out to the community, spread the message of faith, and extend a warm welcome to all who walked through its doors. But what truly distinguished

Parkside Fellowship from other congregations was its commitment to inclusivity and love. Leaders made a special effort to ensure that everyone, regardless of their faith journey, felt welcomed and embraced. The warmth and acceptance were not just acts of human kindness; they were a reflection of the fellowship's dedication to creating a place where all could belong.

The spirit of inclusivity, love, and community extended not just to religious practice but to the wider community as well. Parkside Fellowship was more than a congregation; it was a hub of community engagement, a place where faith met everyday life, and where every action, every endeavour, was rooted in the shared values of acceptance and belonging.

In Parkside Fellowship, I found a place where faith wasn't just preached; it was lived, experienced, and shared. It was a place where diversity was embraced, where faith was a deeply personal journey that was respected, and where the focus was on building not just a congregation but a thriving community of believers.

The spirit of soul-winning and outreach, the commitment to inclusivity and love, and the warmth of the fellowship all echoed the teachings of Christ. This fellowship was more than a place of worship; it was a living embodiment of Christ's enduring presence in the world, and the warmth of its embrace remains etched in my memory as a testament to the enduring power of Jesus' love. I hope that the poem will do justice in giving you a small window into the experience of the joys I felt being a part of a community like Parkside

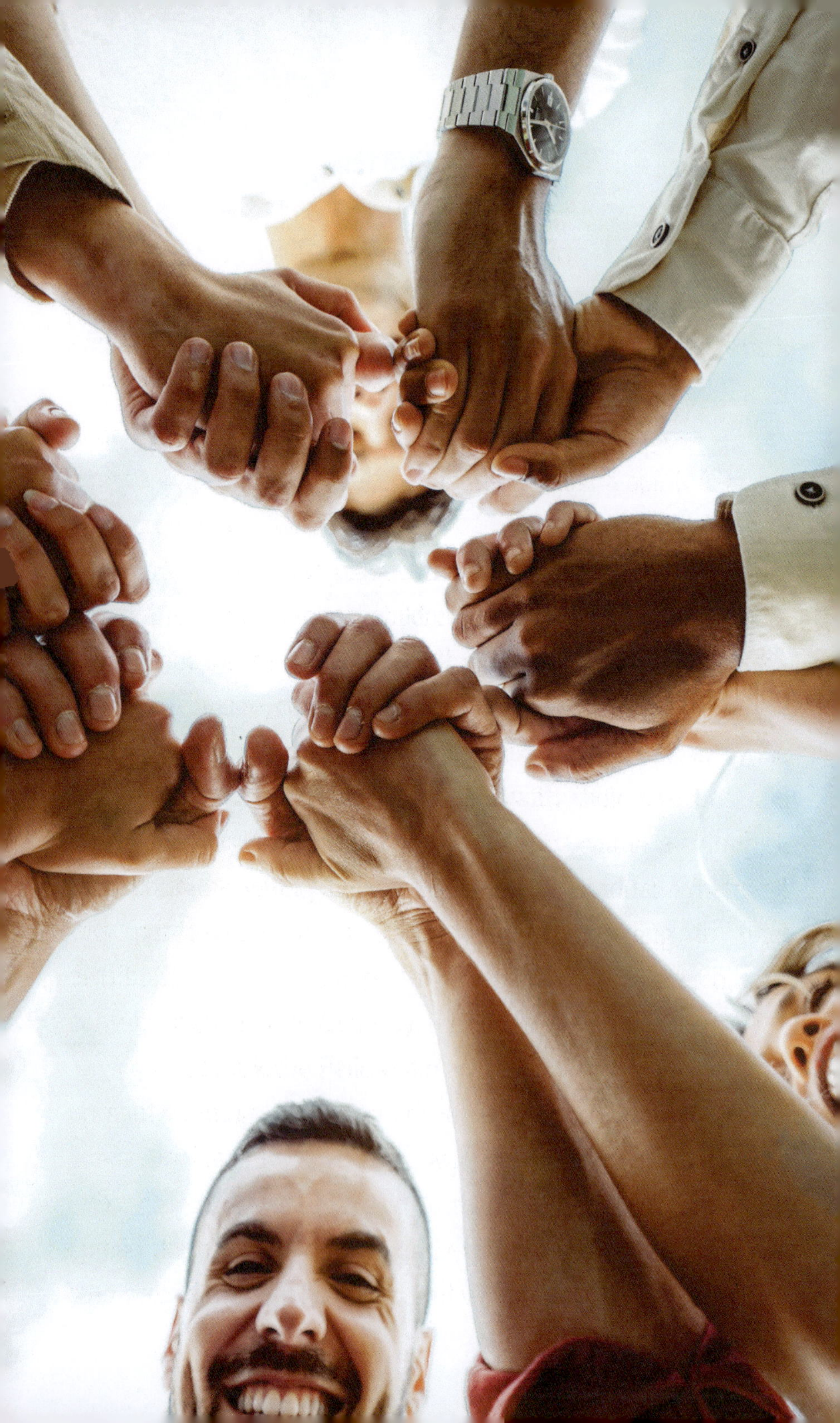

You hear de news bout Parkside fellowship
It's the newest ting pan de Reading market
Dem a people who love Gad
and dem want you fu know
Bringing the community together is de way to go

Ebry Sabbath dem meet
in de reformed church building
Lively discussions and much melodious singing
Dem treat you like family, me nar lie to you
Ask Forace, he will tell you wha me say a true

De one in charge them call him Steve
He short and bald but me a beg you please
What he lack in height he make up in wisdom
Cause even short people will make it to de kingdom

Fellowship lunch there is no lack
When you come once, you want to come back
De fry dumpling sweet, dem mek you heart flatter
Boye dem warm you up – good an prapa

Jam day was an event the youths did organise
People from all over, come to patronise
De day went on without a fuss
Dem youths naym, till dem belly nearly buss

DL wrote a play with Noah's ark –
gave me a fright
Me never know likkle Sammy was so bright
From all karner a eh mouth big words a pop out
Park Side hab talent
Dat you don't even know bout

Dem plan action groups ,to involve de community
Eberybady can be place with an activity
Making de gospel relevant, is what de groups aim to do
So there is an activity for all a aru

So get on board lets sail together
We go mek this community set a fire
A fire that go burn the paths of sin
Reading for Jesus we mus win

## Newbold - I Can't Believe It

The five years my family spent at Newbold while my husband was completing his Undergraduate and Master's programs was truly extraordinary. They were, in many ways, the best years of our lives. We arrived at the college when our son was just five years old. It was a place of discovery, growth, and community like no other.

One of the most cherished aspects of our life there was the freedom and security it offered our son. He could roam the open field and play in the playground with other children, all within the safe confines of the college grounds. It was a joy to watch him build friendships that would last a lifetime, right under our watchful eyes.

For my husband, Newbold provided not just an academic haven but a physical one too. He and his colleagues would often engage in spirited football matches, a form of exercise and a break from the rigours of their assignments. The college's unique setup made this possible. Family housing, consisting of flats, was just a few yards from the main college campus where classes were conducted, ensuring that life and learning coexist harmoniously. Yet, what truly defined our life at the seminary was its diverse and vibrant community. Families from all corners of the globe, hailing from Europe, Africa, the Caribbean, and beyond, found a home in family housing. It was a microcosm of the world's cultures, languages, and traditions.

Friday afternoons especially carried the aroma of this diversity. The air was filled with the scent of an array of cultural cuisines as families prepared for their Sabbath lunches. It was a symphony of flavours that awakened every one of my taste buds, reminding me of the richness of our shared experiences.

As a community, we often came together for more than just meals. We organized social activities that brought families and students in the main college residence together. Sporting events, barbecues, and worship sessions became the threads that wove us into a tight-knit, supportive family. These were the moments that transcended cultural boundaries and fostered a deep sense of togetherness.

It was within this close-knit community, in the heart of family housing, that the inspiration for my next poem was born. We were preparing for a special family service, and I had been asked to contribute a special item. I wanted to capture the essence of what it was like living in family housing and being part of a college fraternity.

Different ideas swirled in my mind, but one particular phrase kept surfacing: 'I can't believe it.' It encapsulated the wonder of our journey, the incredible collage of experiences, and the unspoken joy that filled our days. Once I seized upon that expression, the rest of the poem began to take shape, reflecting the awe and gratitude we felt for the extraordinary life we lived.

For five years we formed lasting friendships and created memories that are eternally carved on my mind. They serve as evidence to the power of community, diversity, and shared experiences, a testament to the sense of 'I can't believe it' that we carry with us.

These years at the Newbold College were a gift. a chapter in our lives that we hold dear, a place where we learned that God's grace and goodness truly know no bounds.

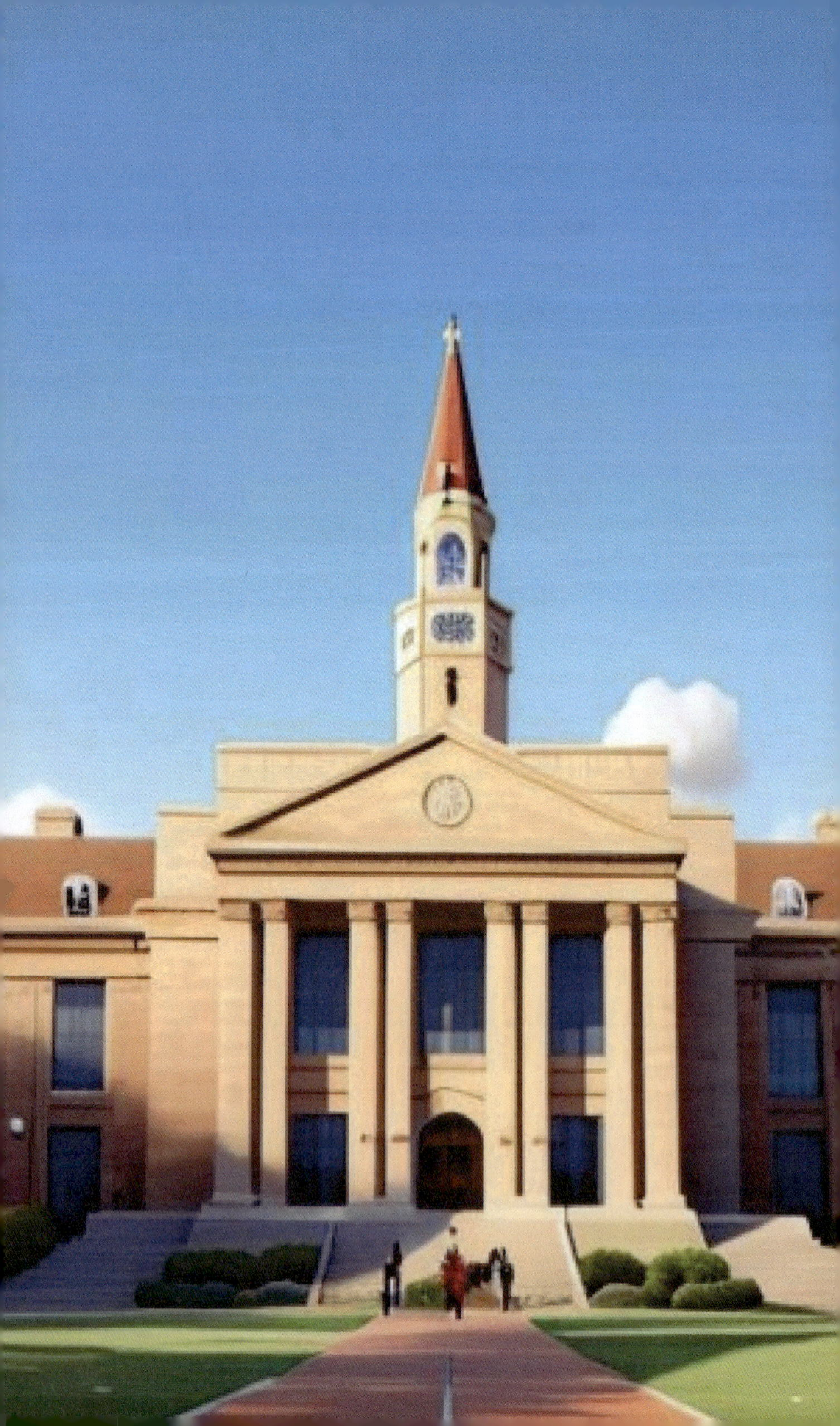

I can't believe it
I said I can't believe it

3 years + 2 don garn a ready
I leaving Newbold for pastures anew
Am still broke
But God will see me through

I remember going to the finance department
Standing with me mouth wide open
Looking at de financial statement
Me put it in the air me put it on de grung
No matter how me put it
dem figures nar come dung

Don't even think bout going to de treasurer
Bout you going to discus de matter
Him will sen you to Patrick to pray
that you financially recover

I can't believe it
I said I can't believe it

Going home to family housing was another ting
Dem carpet ole me a tell you bredrin
But the good Lord heard me lamentin
Dem install new carpets, kitchen and flooring

Dr Phil to de rescue, de children dem say
No more swimming pool when dem come to play
Dem happy how de playground looking nice
De parents dem smiling like them see paradise

We had a bar b que one Sunday, de rain wasn't falling
But there was NJ with one big bawling
Me say boye, wha happen to you?
He said to me – "extended essay hard, na true?"

I can't believe it
I said I can't believe it

Graduation time is finally at hand
I want to look sharp you understand
But when me husband say he name not on de list
Me heart beating fase me adrenalin pumping
I lef fu de college to find out what's happening!

I run to Steve to beg him please
Give me husband a break
After all him human him can make mistake
Give him a chance to do over de paper
And I praying "Lawd let him write a likkle betta"

I can't believe it
I said I can't believe it

Now graduation come and me proud as can be
Me see Sarah, Tony and even sister Wagi
Now walking down de aisle was my huzzie
Me glad me tek time to look after he

Graduates hold you head up high with no regrets
Your hard work and sleepless nights
kept you in check
Be proud that you were part of this great institution
For dis a de place that build solid foundations

You betta believe it
I said you betta believe it

## Leeds District

Leeds, a city I had never set foot in until my husband's pastoral appointment, became a place that I would grow to love deeply. His newfound responsibility was to lead congregations in this diverse and vibrant city. The richness of the culture and the culinary delights of Leeds captured my heart from the very beginning.

Leeds, like many big cities, offered numerous opportunities for work and education. Still, having previously resided in a small village, we knew that bustling city life wasn't quite our cup of tea. Our search for a new home led us to a smaller, close-knit community just outside of Leeds.

This decision turned out to be quite beneficial. My husband had a manageable daily commute of less than an hour, allowing him to serve his congregations while maintaining a healthy work-life balance. It also provided our son with a convenient way to finish his secondary education – he could easily take the bus to school when my husband was unable to carry him. Meanwhile, I was committed to pursuing my university studies full-time, and the proximity of our new home made the daily commute far more manageable.

The transition from a small village to a larger city was

initially daunting, especially considering the recent responsibilities that came with leading larger congregations. We were still relatively new to the role of being a pastoral family, and the abruptness of this change meant we had to adapt quickly or risk feeling overwhelmed.

Our initial introductions to the congregations took place at the main church, which not only had the largest number of parishioners but was also considered the mother church to three smaller congregations. Among the sea of unfamiliar faces, a few were known to us, but the majority were strangers. As time went on, those unfamiliar faces evolved into friends and partners in ministry. The daunting prospect had turned into a welcoming and warm community.

Leeds holds a special place in our hearts. In this city, my faith in God was stretched and challenged in ways it hadn't been before. Our prayer life deepened, and the connections we forged transformed our lives. The assignment in Leeds wasn't just about pastoral responsibilities but personal growth, faith, and community.

And so, in honour of our time and ministry in Leeds, I would like to share a poem that captures the essence of our experiences in this remarkable city.

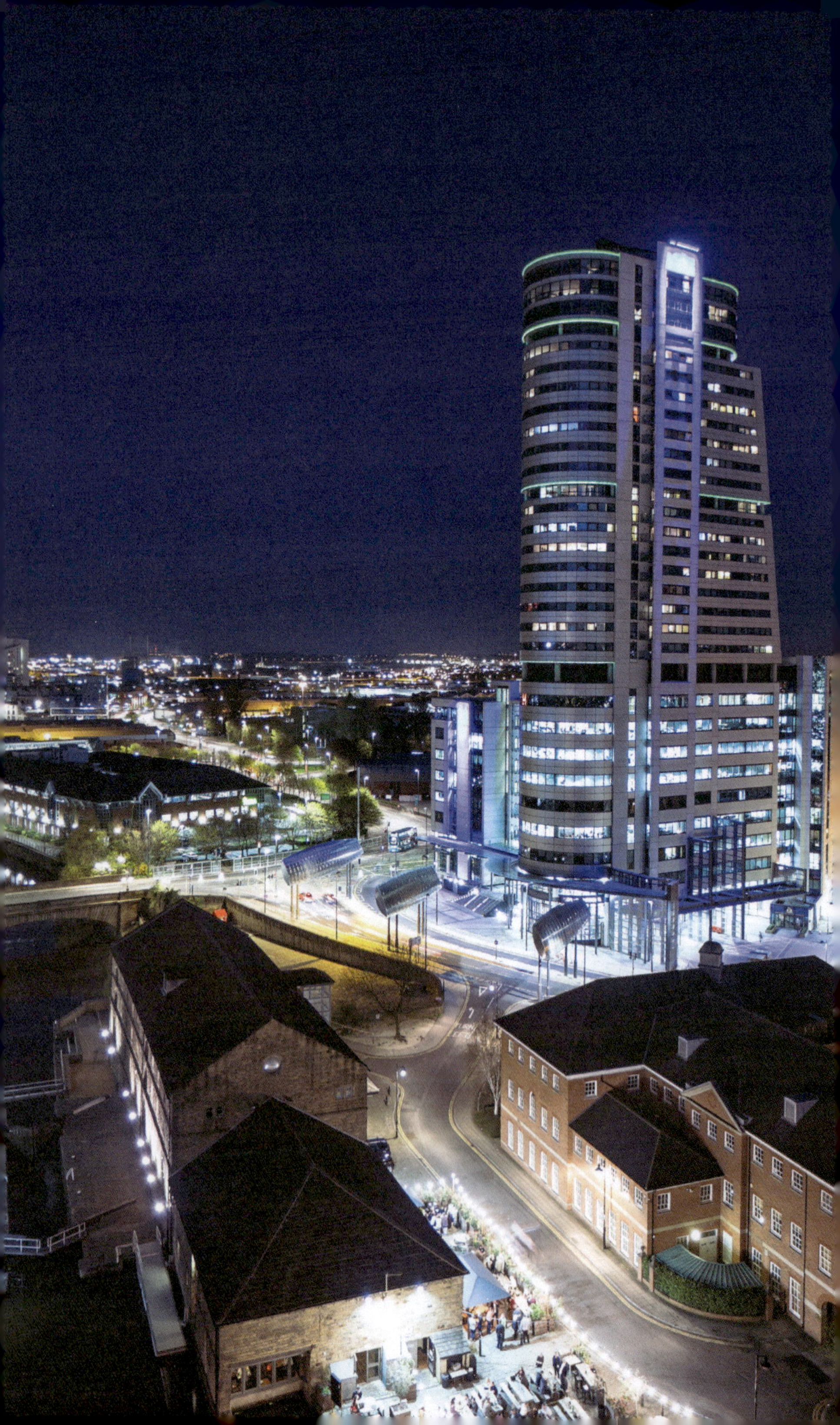

Leeds district, was de news dey did bring
This is where you will be ministering
We came willingly and with an open heart
Promising God that we will do our part


We came to de front fu de intro to tec place
We did shock to see, de whole church in one space
We were not constipated, as many may have thought
Be we did frighten was the feeling it brought


De people dem friendly, warm and kind
But some a dem hard as we did come to fine
Neverdeless our prayer life increase
and our reading too
So we happy an grateful cause we growing
all thanks to aru


The minister is de one them call Sammy G
Is me honey so single ladies, tek ya yie aff a he
Him proud to be pastoring a district such as this
Talent, diversity, and skill all on de list

Pop Brown, from Central is a Caribbean man
Him rice and peas is the best, in de whole a England
Don't talk bout Muzenda and she stew beans
That will make you lick you plate clean! clean!
Mama Fusty jellof rice is tasty to de bite
That can cure even elder Badu's haughty appetite
Sister Miri's greens dem full a iron
Man when you eat them you feel trang like a lion

Our pathfinders and adventurer clubs, are a force to reckon with
They are our future, lets continue to support them forthwith
Adventurers me have a special place, in me heart fu you
Don't tell the pathfinders but me lub dem too

Our ministry here is heartfelt and sincere
Leeds district we love you and we do care
We are happy to be here no matter de circumstance
Gad put you in we path way in advance

So lets enjoy de likkle time we have together
With prayer any storm we can weather
If me squeeze you toe and you get upset
Come talk with me life's too short, to cuss and fret

Leeds for Jesus is our ultimate goal
If we keep our yie pan Jesus His will to unfold
After all, there is only one heaven to gain
So lets make it together in Jesus name

## Unconditional Positive Regard

Being part of a church community can be both challenging and exciting. Nevertheless, my life wasn't solely consumed by church activities; I also enjoyed my university life, which allowed me to pursue my passion for helping those in need. I firmly believe that it's my mission to assist individuals looking for better ways to navigate life. My training in counselling was instrumental in achieving this goal.

Attending university as an adult comes with its advantages and disadvantages. One of the challenges I encountered was managing assignments while taking care of my family simultaneously. It was undoubtedly manageable, but when the assignments took the form of presentations, I found myself wrestling with anxiety. I tended to get tongue-tied and lose focus before and during presentations. With a particular assignment, I was determined to overcome this initial nervousness to earn a passing grade.

I began by delving deep into the topic assigned for our group presentation. I immersed myself in various books, newspaper articles, and journals related to the subject matter. I diligently took notes and began assembling my presentation slides. However, it was through what I can only describe as divine inspiration that a poem began to form in my mind. The experience was almost surreal, and it allowed me to connect with the topic on a much deeper and more personal level. It no longer felt like an academic exercise; it became a profound reflection on the concept of Unconditional Positive Regard (UPR).

UPR is a fundamental requirement for a Person-Centred counsellor, and it's a principle I strive to live by, both within the counselling room and outside. However, this wasn't always the case. There was a time when I struggled to accept people whose values and beliefs were in stark contrast to my own.

The shift in my thinking and behaviour occurred several years prior, during my diploma studies in therapeutic counselling. It was during this time that I learned that accepting someone for who they are doesn't necessarily mean agreeing with or condoning their lifestyle. This shift in perspective transformed the way I approached my interactions with others.

I knew that I had to present my poem to the rest of my group for it to be considered as part of our collective presentation. I approached the other group members with a sense of apprehension. The fact that the poem was not written in standard English added to my concerns. However, to my relief, the group members not only understood the message conveyed by the poem but also embraced it wholeheartedly. It became the highlight of our presentation, the element that tied everything together. As a group, we received a passing grade. I'm not claiming that the poem alone achieved this, but it marked a significant turning point for me.

As you read and reflect on the message conveyed by this poem, my hope is that you, too, will realize that accepting people for who they are is the first step in fostering understanding and compassion. It's a lesson that has transformed my perspective and, in many ways, the way I interact with the world around me.

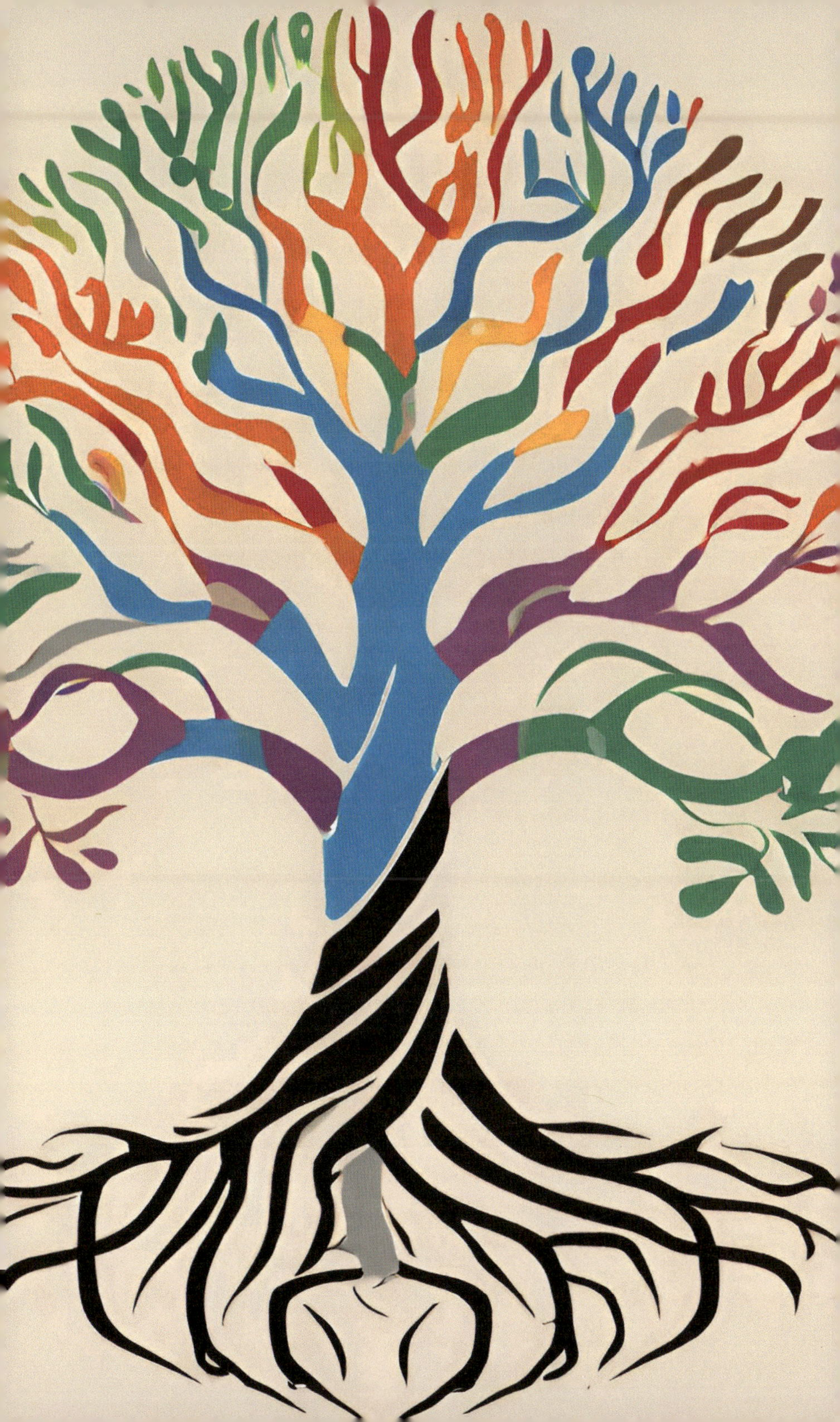

Unconditional Positive Regard
de Rogerians dem say
Is de attitude to adapt in the person-centred maelay
It's a hard thing to practice you will agree wit me
because some a de behaviour is far from savoury

But acceptance, is de ting you want to project
Even if you want to tell de client which road fu tec
It all bout dem it not bout arwe
So accept dem fu who dem really be
Show dem that you care and care unconditionally
For this is de way that UPR will work successfully

Put no conditions on de way dem must present
Preacher, prisoner, or plumber whomever they represent
No mind that de client say you nice
and want to get with you
Reciprocate that behaviour and de association will have you fu true

But if that don't happen and you think you get off scotts free
Your conscience will have you an from that, there is no empaty

Counsellors listen to me and let me fortell
UPR is not just for therapy but for home as well
Respect yourself and the client will ring the bell
That you are a professional at heart not just for a spell

## Boy Chile

Boy Chile was penned as a heartfelt tribute to a young graduate on the cusp of adulthood, a momentous occasion that deserved not only celebration but also recognition of the profound significance it held. It was a day that exuded pride, not just for his family, but for the entire community. A jubilant gathering of friends and relatives came together, feasting on an abundant spread that filled not only their stomachs but also their hearts with a sense of accomplishment and hope.

In a world that often paints a bleak picture of black boys, casting them as 'time wasters' or stereotyping them in ways that do not reflect their true potential. This event offered an opportunity to shatter those misconceptions. It became a platform to express the truth about our black boys, not as society might perceive them, but as the bright, ambitious, and resilient individuals they truly are.

Initially, I contemplated crafting a poem to convey this message, but as so often happens, divine inspiration took the reins. As I listened to that inner voice, the seed of an idea took root and began to germinate. It grew into a piece of work that I am genuinely proud of.

For me, as a mother of a 'boy chile,' this poem transcends a mere celebration of a university graduation. It captures thetransformation of a BLACK boy into a man, a journey that offers the promise of breaking free from the shackles of prejudice and injustice through the power of education. It is a testament to a young man's growth and his emergence as a force of resilience and wisdom in a world that doesn't always offer an equal playing field.

Education, as I've come to know, is a formidable tool that, if used wisely, can be the key to unlocking a world of opportunities. It's a means to combat not just poverty but also idleness, and the path to personal empowerment. If you, too, are reading this as a parent of a boy chile, I urge you to instil in him the profound importance of a sound education. It's not merely about degrees or diplomas; education transcends the confines of textbooks and assignments.

To educate our 'boy chile' is to equip him with the knowledge to discern right from wrong, to make choices that reflect his values and beliefs, and to understand that every decision he makes carries consequences. It's about nurturing a sense of justice and empathy and teaching him to stand up for what he believes is right. In a world that's often filled with injustice, educating our boy chile is about preparing him to be a beacon of change, a force for good, and a torchbearer of progress.

In this journey, fathers hold a pivotal role. They bear the responsibility to lead by example, to guide and mentor, and to demonstrate the values that our boy chile should embrace. Their presence and influence are instrumental in shaping the men

they will become. I hope that "Boy Chile" serves as not just a poem but as a
source of encouragement, a reminder of the importance of education, a call to action for parents, and a testament to the potential that lies within every black boy. May you find within these words the motivation to nurture and support the growth of your own 'boy chile' and to celebrate the unique journey that education can provide.

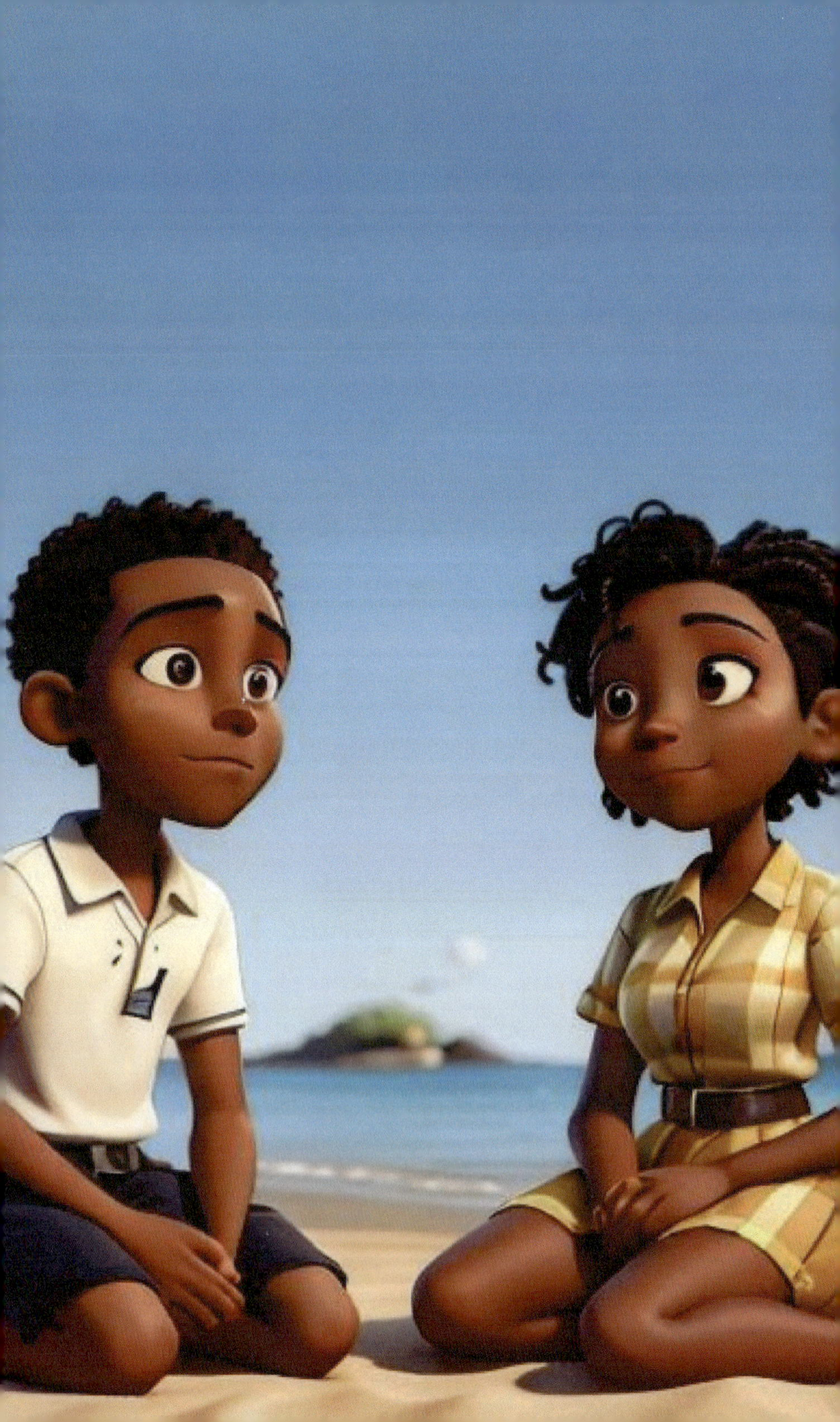

Boy Chile you garn and Mek you parents proud
Setting yourself apart from de rest a de croud
Studying hard to get de likkle paper
A step up on de success ladder

Boy chile a good education will be with you forever
Aim high and look back you will never
Forget de girls for now and how dem look sweet
Someday your sugar dumplin you will meet

Boy Chile, don't be like dem boys ,on de street karna
Smoking de weed that ting dem call ganja
It will only mess wit you mind and bring suffering
Keep away from it, you hear me darlin?

Boy chile look at you pupa him is one to emulate
Him is treasurer which take a likkle faith
Its not he good looks that land him that position
It's the grace of God and him sound education

Education is not just bout being book smart
Its bout making choices that set you apart
Studiation beat education me granny did say
So boy chile study hard, rest and play

A life of injustice you may not be able to escape
But the values you hold put ya life in shape
Learn boy chile what is passed on by you pupa
He was once where you were and had it harder

You life has a purpose ask God what it is about
Listen to Him and you will find out
Him lub you more than you will ever know
Serve him boy chile you will reap what you sow

## De Pastor's Wife

De Pastor's Wife emerged from a pivotal phase in my life, a time when I grappled with an identity crisis. It was the moment my husband, after much soul-searching, embraced his divine calling to become a minister. To say that I was consumed by fear about the path ahead would be an understatement. I was gripped by uncertainty, unsure of what my new role would entail. The weight of expectation felt crushing.

During this internal turmoil, a wise friend offered a simple yet profound piece of advice: "Be yourself." It seemed like a straightforward directive, but the simplicity of the words masked the profound impact they would have on the course of my life. I initially thought that being the pastor's wife came with a set of expectations. I believed that I should possess a beautiful singing voice, perhaps play a musical instrument with grace, and attend every church function with a perpetual smile fixed on my face.

As years passed, I gradually grasped the profound truth that it was not just okay but essential to be authentic. I didn't need to conform to the expectations of others or mould myself into someone I wasn't. Their vision of who I should be didn't have to dictate how I lived my life. Authenticity became my guiding principle, and living by the dictates of others would mean living a lie.

I understood that I wasn't always serious, and there were moments when I indulged in silliness, embracing the joy of laughter without reservation.

As it turned out, my favourite musical instrument wasn't the piano but the bass guitar. Not that I can play either, but who said I needed to be able to play an instrument as the pastor's wife? I discovered immense pleasure in dancing to the rhythm of my much-loved gospel artists, my hands raised high during worship, my heart unburdened by concerns about what others might think. Reclaiming 'me' was liberating, a breath of fresh air in a world that often tries to shape us into predetermined moulds.

During this journey, I pursued my dream of becoming a fully qualified counsellor with my private practice, a demonstration of the belief that we have the power to shape our identities and that our sense of self does not have to remain static.

For instance, I used to be shy and not very assertive. However, my professional life demanded assertiveness, and I realized that shyness would not hold me back. With time, I learned to break free from those self-imposed limitations and assert myself confidently.

If my story resonates with your struggles with identity, know that your journey can also have a positive outcome. I found solace in turning to the One who knows me best and loves me most—God. He reminded me that my ultimate identity rests in Him, and I need not allow others to define who I should be. Instead, I have chosen to reveal my authentic self to the world.

I've come to understand that I am precious in God's eyes, and people will form their own opinions of me. But that's perfectly fine because, at the end of the day, I am being true to myself. The journey of embracing authenticity and reclaiming our true selves is a liberating one. It's a journey that not only brings us closer to our essence but also resonates with others who are on a similar path. It's a journey that testifies to the power of self-discovery and the transformative impact of being genuine in a world that sometimes pressures us to conform. Embrace your uniqueness, celebrate your journey, and be unapologetically you.

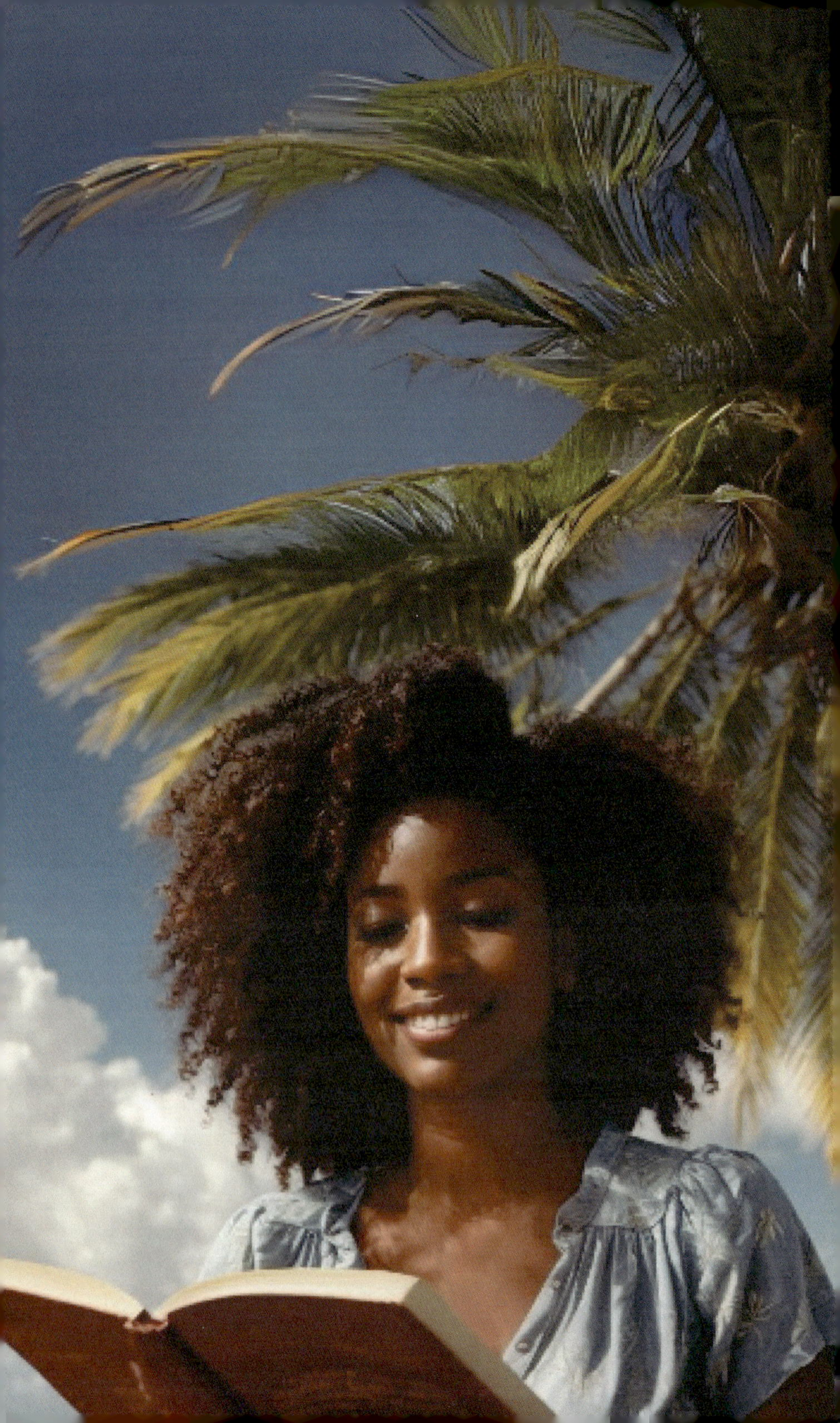

De pastor wife watching me hard you see
It was so intense de way she looking pan me
Me check me clothes but them was fine
So surely de fault could not be mine

So me decide fu ask she, what's de matter?
Why she looking at me without a batter batter?
She say being de pastor's wife is a hard calling
Putting up with all de demands can be so exhausting

She say she carn play de piano
or even the organ too
Writing sermons and story telling
is not what she likes to do
But de expectation sometimes a de problem to note
And trying hard fu please ebrybady is no joke

And don't talk bout what dem say
bout she pickney them
She get so vex she ask if they feeding them?
Dem say pks (pastors' kids) should be always polite and never in doubt
But dem is angels? So wha dem a talk bout?

She say she husband treat she well,
and understand she plight
He tell she honey, be youself
and everything will be alright
But it's so hard to please some people you meet
It's either you dress too short
or them na lub ya teeth!

She tell me bout Sister Mavis
the one that sing off key
Engage she in singing lessons all fu free
Sister Mavis a bellow all kine a decibel
De singing lesson was not going very well

She thank sister Mavis fu wa she try fu do
but she a no singer lets get that straight!
God give she other talents that she learn to appreciate

During de conversation, de Pastor wife stop fu think
But a one woman she be, she nar no duppy
How can dem expect she fu be all them smaddy?
She lok pan me from head to toe

Then shout with an echo, nothing tall a go so

She decide to bring de conversation to an end
She realise that she unique from way back when
She say she a Shirley pickney
She a no liability
So being the pastor's wife is jus part a she identity

Turn the page for a Surprise
Addition

The following is a skit I wrote for children between the ages of 9 and 12 years old. I find great satisfaction and fulfilment in working with children. My devotion to children has allowed my creative talents to come alive through presentations, skits and plays I believe I am at my best creative self when writing skits

# Am Nobody's Fool

**Narrator:** The stage is set in a vibrant schoolyard where a group of friends is gathered. Meet Frank, a spirited young boy with a desire for lively discussions, and his friends—Roy, Margaret, Patricia, Thora, and Telmargorie. Little did they know that a seemingly ordinary day would take a surprising turn, unveiling a challenge that would test their bonds and beliefs. The scene begins with Frank pacing and muttering to himself.

**Frank:** Am I de fool or a he de fool? But me carn be de fool – or me just fooling me self? No, no, no, no, me a nobody's fool.

[Roy, Patricia and Margaret enter the scene]

**Roy:** Frank, who are you talking to?

**Frank:** Nobody, me just discussing a very troublesome matter with me self.

**Margaret:** Well, I guess it's ok to talk to yourself, but when you start answering back, that might be a problem. So talk to us instead.

**Frank:** Ok, you know Melvin de new boye that joined we school last week?

**Patricia:** Yes, what about him?

**Frank:** Well, de teacher ask me to sit with him and introduce him to some a aru.

**Patricia:** So what's wrong with that?

**Frank:** Notton, but when we dey have lunch me start praying fu me food as usual. De boye look pan me and say na badder pray because none Gad dey.

[Others gasp and look surprised]

**All:** He said what?

**Frank:** Ya hear me a tell you, him say no Gad dey.

[Thora and Telmargorie enters]

**Margaret:** Wow! This is serious!

**Telmargorie:** Thora and I could not help overhearing the conversation. Did Melvin really say that there is no God?

**Frank:** The las time me check me mouth na full a wata, me say, de boye say no Gad dey.

**Thora:** By the way, Frank, why are you wearing those dark glasses?

**Frank:** Aah eh, notton, me haffu go now.

**Patricia:** Frank, stop!

**Frank:** Look! Me hab things to do, me haffu go now.

**Thora:** Why are you in such a rush?

**Patricia:** Take your glasses off so we can see your eyes.

**Telmargorie:** Oooh my friend, someone got you really good.

**Frank:** Ok, listen let me tell you de hole story. Memba me tell you that Melvin say that no Gad dey, right? Ya with me?

**Roy:** Yeah?

**Frank:** Him say de reason why no Gad dey a because he cannot see him.

**Patricia:** And he hit you for that?

**Frank:** No.

**Margaret:** Come on, Frank, tell us the rest of the story.

**Frank:** Me tell him me believe that wan Gad dey because only Gad can mek Ian get 100 percent pan de spelling test we did last week.

**Margaret:** Hmmm, that's true, we know that Ian is not a strong speller.

**Frank:** Trang speller? Ian for years was spelling him own name with a G'

**Roy:** Ok Frank continue

**Frank:** I have a fren call Collin, he could thief de seed from the mango while you still eating it but Gad save he and now him nar do them things no more, so me know that wan Gad dey.

**Patricia:** Absolutely!

**Thora:** And then Melvin hit you?

**Frank:** No, him just laugh atta me.

**Patricia:** Then he hit you?

**Frank:** No, I remember that me daddy did tell me and me bredda one time in family worship that a fool says in his heart there is no Gad.

**Telmargorie:** Yes, it says so in Psalms chapter 14 verse one.

**Frank:** Thats right Temargorie. So me call him a fool.

**All:** You did what!!

**Frank:** Ya hear me, me call him a fool and THEN he hit me.

**Thora:** Am so sorry you had to go through that. It was not right for Melvin to hit you. Violence is not ok.

**Roy:** Guys, I have an idea, why don't we pray about it and ask God to help Frank to say the right things to Melvin when he speaks to him again?

**Frank:** Me, I must talk to Melvin again?

**Roy:** Yes Frank he needs to know that what he did to you was wrong and you can talk to him about God. Don't worry we can go with you.

**Margaret:** That's a good idea, let's pray right now.

[As the children huddle together to pray for Frank, Melvin walks by]

**Thora:** Hey, isn't that Melvin?

**Frank:** Where? – hide me.

**Margaret:** Don't be afraid, Frank.

**Patricia:** Melvin looks like he is in pain.

**Frank:** What a gwarn Melvin, wha wrong wid you?

**Melvin:** I don't feel well, I have a headache.

**Frank:** Me sarrie fu hear that, let me see ya headache?

**Melvin:** Don't be silly, you can't see my headache.

**Frank:** Well let me touch it then?

**Melvin:** You can touch my head but you can't touch my headache

**Frank:** But how you know it dey?

**Melvin:** Because I feel it, hey wait a minute!

**Margaret:** That's right, Melvin, you cannot see or touch the pain from your headache, but you know it's there because you can feel it.

**Patricia:** That's what Frank was trying to tell you when he told you about the existence of God.

**Roy:** You may not be able to see Him or touch Him, but you know he's there because so many things around you tell you God is real.

**Telmargorie:** If you like you could come along to one of our bible studies for kids at church. The Pastor is very nice and he explains the bible in a simple way for us to understand.

**Thora:** He also makes the study fun and interesting but first I think you owe Frank an apology for hitting him.

**Melvin:** You are right, Frank please forgive me for hitting you that was not a nice thing to do and I am very sorry.

**Frank:** Me forgive you

**Melvin:** I would love to attend your bible study and maybe I have been a fool.

**All:** You've been a what?

**Melvin:** You heard me, I have been a fool, but no more. Am nobody's fool!

# Glossary

| Words | Meaning |
| --- | --- |
| Likkle | Little |
| Tek | Take |
| Betta | Better |
| De | The |
| Bawling | Crying |
| Naym | Eating/eat |
| Smaddy | People |
| Ebry | Every |
| Aru | You/everyone |
| Fu | For/to |
| Yie | Eye |
| Trang | Strong |
| Maelay | Story |
| Haffu | Have to |
| Sarrie | Sorry |
| Croud | Crowd |
| Karna | Corner |
| Wit | With |
| Respon | Respond |
| Eh | His |
| Jus | Just |
| Not me sa | Not me |
| Suffa | Suffer |

| | |
|---|---|
| Pan | On |
| Mek | Make |
| Dem | Them |
| Lawn | Lord |
| Na | Don't |
| Nar | Not/won't |
| Boye | Boy |
| Prapa | Proper |
| Buss | Burst |
| Garn | Gone |
| Grung | Ground |
| Huzzie | Husband |
| Aff | Off |
| Lub | Love |
| Notton | Nothing |
| Puppa | Father |
| Bredda | Brother |
| Member | Remember |
| Gad | God |
| Wonda | Wonder |

## About the Author

*Roxan Gardner is a trained Counsellor by profession with her private practice (REG Counselling Service). She believes her experience, knowledge and training have given her the ability to work with a wide range of issues, including low self-worth, abuse, anxiety and depression. She is passionate about her profession and is confident that although the journey's first step may be painful, it is the first step that will lead to restoration, healing and wholeness.*

*When she is not engaging with clients, she enjoys supporting her husband in Pastoral Ministry. Roxan and Pastor Gardner have co-authored several devotional books. Roxan's passion is to live life to the full while being a blessing to those she is privileged to serve.*